GPS
M Y
Success

The Address You Input in Life Determines Your Destination

Book Coach – The Self-Publishing Maven
Cover Design – Okomota
Interior Design – Istvan Szabo, Ifj, Sapphire Guardian Publishing

ISBN: 978-1-7343674-0-9

www.karimellis.com

GPS
MY
Success

The Address You Input in Life Determines Your Destination

KARIM R. ELLIS
Foreword by Les Brown

T

DEDICATION

I was told that you knew me before I entered my mother's womb. That the specific reason for my birth was well thought out before I developed mental awareness of it. That my purpose on this planet was predestined prior to my arrival. And till this exact moment I have been gravitating towards. At first, I was unaware. My unique gifts and talents would literally come to life in the right arenas. My personality would magnetically pull me towards certain things. At times I'd appear not to fit in never knowing this was all by grand design.

It's been a long road that I've traveled. At times I'd have friends, family, and companionship. At other times I'd be all alone. But throughout the setbacks, the disappointment and the losses I knew you were there. Watching over me. Guiding me. Challenging me to hang in there and finish the race. To remain consistent while pursuing the higher calling of excellence. And so after fast forwarding many years into the future, here we are.

It is to my Heavenly Father that I dedicate this book.

I thank you not only for the journey and the people resources that have helped to shape this vision but also for never giving up on me. I thank you as well for all of the people you have allowed my story, insight, and wisdom to positively impact on this walk. I can never fully repay you for all that you done. I just want to say that I love you. I appreciate you. And most importantly of all, I will continue to run this race and not let you down.

Thank you.

I want my story to positively impact others!

ACKNOWLEDGEMENTS

Les Brown
Brianah Ellis
Delatorro McNeal
Harold Carson
Ona Brown
Charles Cary
John Ellis
Apollo Ellis
Fendi Ellis
Pastor Freddie Piphus
Miyah Hipsher

Bobby Ellis Sr.
Jimmy Leo
Vashti Carson
Dr. Valerie Parker
Byron Nelson
Kaaree Hipsher
Aries Ellis
Team No Sleep
Lenai Hipsher
Imani Hipsher

FOREWORD

I am a person who loves life; every day, I wake up with excitement because I am committed to living my dreams with passion until I exit this thing called life. This has me in a constant state of discovery to uncover the various ways to "live fully and die empty."

Time is our most valuable resource. Our goals, visions, hopes, and dreams have an expiration date that ends when we do. More and more people leave this world with regret because they never pursued their passions while they were physically able.

Karim Ellis delivered "GPS My Success" at one of my events, and I believed the message was so unique, radical, and powerful, it needed to be transformed from his motivational keynote presentation into a book; this book you now hold in your hands.

I count Karim Ellis, as not just a mentee, but as a protege and a personal friend. We have traveled together and have spoken on many platforms and stages. Karim is a personal development expert, certified corporate leadership trainer, and a master speaking coach who specializes in cutting through your red tape to help you unlock your version 2.0, so you can achieve massive success.

He uses public speaking, teaching, coaching, training, workshops, and social media channels to reach those who need his help the most. Organizations such as Honda, Ford, General Electric, Anthem, the US Military, the United States Postal Service, and many more have experienced Karim and his "GPS My Success" presentation, and now, he brings his expertise to you in his book, *GPS My Success*.

Many testimonials on Karim's YouTube channel and website speak on his ability to help people transform their lives. These testimonials are proof of people leaving their comfort zone and using his success principles to create businesses, chase their dreams, and create wealthy lifestyles, as well as individuals climbing the corporate ladder.

GPS My Success directs readers to identify the right vision with clear concise goals; the same way a car's GPS directs a driver to navigate unknown roads to a final destination. You will learn with whom and what you need to strategically connect to obtain faster results, while navigating past the pitfalls and dream killers.

 Do you want to spend two-thirds of your life working on someone else's dream, or do you want to live a life of greatness? This book gives you the blueprint to devise your game plan while teaching you to look for and leverage all your external and internal resources. Why wait? Start now, using easy to understand steps, illustrations, and a few hidden gems to motivate and inspire you on your journey to success. The world is waiting for you to bring out the GREATNESS that is within you.

- Les Brown
The Motivator/Mamie Brown's Baby Boy

TABLE OF CONTENTS

INTRODUCTION
WHY GPS?

You know, I've been a very blessed man. I've traveled all across this country. I've met and built relationships with some of the most amazing people in the world. I've spoken in large cities and small towns, huge auditoriums and small churches. And of all the things I learned, of all the tools I came to rely on, the one thing I use consistently more than anything else—more than my cell phone, even—is my GPS. No matter where I go or who I bring this message to, one thing is always the same; I have to figure out where I'm going, and then I have to get there; otherwise, I'm just going to be talking to myself. So, I plug in the directions, and this little navigational sidekick does all the work for me.

What if life had something like that? Wouldn't it be great if we could just plug our dreams into a Life GPS and watch directions spill out onto some screen, telling us exactly what to do and where to turn to achieve them.

My friend, I'm here to tell you, you already have such a machine *inside* you; you just haven't heard about it yet. You see, a GPS needs five very specific things to get you from where you are to where you want to end up:

1. A destination address
2. Clear concise directions
3. Connectivity and no dead zones
4. The ability to recalculate
5. A well reviewed history log

In this book, I'm going to break these down and show you how they parallel in your life; how properly using your Life GPS can propel you down a path to achieving your goals and dreams. I think about it as an interconnected system, and I call it "GPS Your Success." It's like a vision machine with only one mission: manifest your dreams into reality.

IMPORTANT:

Some of the chapters in this book have "deeper dive" videos associated with them that will allow you the reader to gain a deeper understanding into the messages taught in this book. You can gain access to these videos by texting the word **GPS** to the number **484848**. An online access code will be sent back upon receipt of your text. We ask that you not share this access code with anyone as your purchasing of the book is proof that you are fully invested in your success. Please enjoy the videos.

CHAPTER ONE
PLUG IN THE RIGHT ADDRESS

Where there is no vision, the people perish.
- King Solomon

I find myself in new towns all the time traveling for events. Some are really easy to navigate. Sometimes getting to my speaking gig is as simple as walking down the hall of the conference center I'm staying at. And sometimes the hotel I'm in is opposite the church I'm going to be speaking at. I love those situations. I love not having to wade out into heavy traffic on strange roads in a busy city. But sometimes, that can't be avoided. Sometimes, heavy traffic on strange roads is exactly what my passion calls for. So, what do I do in those situations? You guessed it—I fire up my GPS and plug in that address.

Do you use a GPS? I hope you do. It's a marvel of modern technology, and it has revolutionized travel. Gone are the days of hauling 50-pound atlases across the country with you. All you need is that tiny little box suctioned to your dashboard. And once you plug in that address, everything works like magic, doesn't it? And nowadays it's more convenient than ever before. If you're new to the GPS game, you probably don't even remember that separate box you'd mount on your dash or window. All the technology you need comes stocked right in your smart phone. Just call up the app, type in the destination, and watch it work.

But what if you don't plug in the address? What happens if you're carrying around all this amazing technology, and you forget to tell it where you want to go? Nothing, right? The machine doesn't know where you want to go, and so it doesn't give you any directions — all that innovation…wasted.

I know what you're thinking. *Of course it doesn't! The GPS can't take you anywhere unless you tell it where to take you. Everybody knows that, and that's why no one in their right mind would* not *plug in the address. Why are you wasting my time?*

Here's the truth, and I've seen it countless times. I struggled with this myself for a long time (we're going to discuss that a lot in this book). While you're right—everyone *does* know you must plug in directions to go anywhere with GPS—I still meet people everywhere who don't know the same thing applies to their *life*, and they're just not using it.

I find that people, for the most part, know what their dreams are. This isn't always true, but usually when I ask people what they would do if they could do anything, they generally have an answer. They know they want to build that startup, write that novel, develop that craft, change the world in that amazing way. They know *what* they want to do. So, clearly that's not the problem.

The problem is they don't think about those dreams in a real, actionable way. They don't take the time to reflect, to plug those dreams into their Life GPS in an intentional way, so their mind can manifest those realities for them.

And because they don't, their Life GPS fills up with all sorts of other things by default—pay the bills, mow the lawn, do the work, get the job done.

Look, those things are all fine and good, my friend. Those things are important, and in fact, may be steps on the way to your dreams. But those things are where you are *now*, not where you're *going*. Your mind is a powerful thing, but unless you take the time to give it the direction it needs, it won't know where you want to go. And just like the GPS in your car without any directions, it won't take you anywhere.

So that's step one. It's the most basic, and yet an often-overlooked beginning to manifesting your dreams into reality. You have to get real with yourself. You have to allow yourself to go there. You must quiet your mind so it's just you and your dreams in there, and then you have to plug in the right address to make those dreams a reality.

> *Driving while distracted is a great way*
> *to kill a dream. Stay focused.*
> - Karim Ellis

Another reason it's so important to put an address inside your Life GPS is that it helps you to both identify and avoid distractions. When people fail to achieve their goals in life, many times it isn't because they aren't aiming at the right things; it's because they aren't able to identify the things *keeping* them from success. Things that draw them in the wrong direction or keep them distracted during the course of the battle—and believe me, it is a battle. But when you give your GPS an address, it goes a long way to keeping you on track through those distractions. Later in this book we'll go into a little more detail about clarity and how to move with clarity, but let's spend some time now on the concept of distractions.

Here are three scenarios from my own personal life where I allowed myself to get distracted, showing how those distractions delayed me from achieving my goals. These could happen to anyone reading this book—I hear *many* similar stories at speaking gigs.

The first happened when I was sixteen years old. I had a meeting with my high school guidance counselor about what I intended to do with the rest of my life. I'd been able to skip first grade a young kid, going right into second grade. So I was always one of the youngest kids in my grade, but I was also one of the smartest. My guidance counselor said, "Look, you're getting ready to graduate. Do you have any idea what you want to do with your life? Not what degree do you want to get, or what career do you want to end up in, but what do you want the rest of your life to be like?"

That was a really big question, and it stands out in my mind now, all these years later, as one of the first times I really stopped to think about my future in a long-term way. I spent a good deal of time over the course of that year doing what I call Future Mapping. I sat down and really dove deep into what type of life I wanted. Eventually, I broke my future life down into three areas I knew would always be important to me:

First, I knew I wanted to end up in a job I was happy with. I saw so many adults around me going through the motions in jobs they were miserable in, and I knew I wanted to avoid that like the plague. At the same time, I had felt from an early age I was called to be a speaker. I didn't even know what I wanted to speak about—better yet, what people would *pay* me to speak about. But I knew without a doubt I wanted to be a speaker as part of my profession. In my senior year I was voted "most talkative," and had actually gotten in trouble many times for talking when I wasn't supposed to, so I knew it was something that had been with me pretty much from the womb.

The second part of my Future Mapping was that, even at seventeen, I knew I wanted to be married. You're probably thinking, *that's pretty early in the whole life game to be thinking about marriage,* but I knew even then. I knew I wanted a beautiful wife—someone on the supermodel side of the spectrum. Don't judge; I was very young at the time. I knew I wanted to add three beautiful kids to that picture, and the two-story house with the white picket fence. I wanted to have two or three dogs and live here in Ohio. Specific, yes. But for me, that was the American dream.

My third Future Mapping point was seeing myself as a real estate entrepreneur. I had grown up in a real estate family. My father had owned and sold several properties, and I knew the power of residual income from owning rental properties.

So, there I was at seventeen years old, with three very specific goals:

1. Be a speaker of some description
2. Have a knockout wife and the whole American dream package, and
3. Generate residual income through real estate.

Fast-forward a few years: I'm twenty, and something odd was about to happen. I was enrolled in school and an opportunity came my way. I was offered a job at a medical benefits company, dealing with benefits administration-- basically; we handled the medical benefits for different business clients. When they hired me, I would start at $14/hour. Not a huge amount of money by today's standards, but back then it was at least twice the minimum wage. As a young college student, I was pretty happy with that. And there were a lot of other things to love about the offer. I would be guaranteed 40 hours per week, with paid time off and a 401K with a 100% match right out of the gate. They had a tuition reimbursement program. I would have weekends off. And best of all—a great parking spot and a cubicle with a fantastic view overlooking that parking spot. At that time in my life, all those things sounded wonderful. So, I took the position.

I suspect you know where this is heading. Without going into all the details—it didn't work out in the long run. Year one at the company was great. Year two, I began to struggle. Year three, things were on the ropes. And in year four...I got fired. So, what in the world could be so bad about a job—which four years earlier had been the cat's meow—that could cause me to lose morale so quickly and begin to flake? Hold onto that question; we'll come back to it in a minute.

Scenario #2: I mentioned I wanted to be married. So, I was actively looking for the love of my life. And at the age of twenty-six, I ran across this young lady. She was absolutely beautiful, athletic, great personality—everything was on point. Things started out great...but they didn't stay that way. We dated for 3-4 months, and then everything fell apart.

Remember that American dream I had? Hers was the exact opposite. I wanted to stay in Ohio; she wanted to move out to California and build a fitness company. I wanted kids; she wasn't about to do anything to destroy those six-pack abs. Picket fence, two or three dogs? Nope, she wasn't having it. She wanted a penthouse garage overlooking the city. So, the relationship fell completely apart.

But here's the thing; everything else in the relationship was great. The day-to-day was great. We had awesome chemistry. We enjoyed doing similar things. We could talk freely about anything. So why couldn't we overcome those other differences? Hold that thought, too.

Scenario #3: around the same time I thought I'd found my dream girl, I ran into a guy pushing a Multilevel Marketing company. These companies are all about generating passive or residual income from your downline. You recruit other people into the company, they become part of your downline, and you make residual income off *their* work for a lifetime. Remember, residual income was a big part of my envisioned journey—creating wealth outside of the 9-to-5.

So, I jumped in, fronting $300 to join. Then I started buying their products and services, racking up another thousand dollars' worth of investment in the company. I went to four or five different conferences over the course of 3-4 years—to the tune of about $500 apiece, counting travel and expenses. And then in the fourth year, one of the top people in the company got into fraud trouble and everything came crashing down. I discovered a lot of MLM companies end up that way; but at 26 and just going into the business, I was a bit naïve. And after all my investment and four years of trying to build something, I had nothing to show for it.

Let's rewind now. Each of these scenarios fell apart on the one-yard line. But *why* did they fall apart? What was the problem? What were the issues that couldn't be overcome? You could certainly point to specific negative aspects of each. Conflicting relationship goals, corporate burnout, dealing with a company that turned out to have shady leadership. All of those are true. But the fact is, I should have *never had to deal with any of them.*

What really happened in each of these scenarios is that *I didn't avoid distractions.* I had plugged pretty clear goals into my Future Map, but then had allowed my life to go into completely different directions.

Remember Scenario #1: the great job with all the benefits. Let's be honest: if my goal was to end up as a paid professional speaker—even if I didn't yet know what my topic was going to be—what did that job offer to help me walk into that arena? Nothing. It didn't help me practice that skill set. It didn't help me add to my existing talents. It didn't bring me any relevant education. It didn't help me make connections to that end. In short, it didn't move the needle toward my life's goal at all. The job was a paycheck —nothing more, nothing less. If I had plugged "Paid Professional Speaker" into my Life GPS, I would not have considered that job a route to that address; I would have seen it as a distraction before I ever walked through the door, before the second interview. So why was I there for four years? Because I'd been vague with the address in my Life GPS and allowed myself to be sidelined with distractions.

How about Scenario #2? My goal was to settle down, marry, my American Dream. But the moment I knew this woman's Future Map diverged radically from my own, why didn't I move on? I've seen many people do this same thing; they know what they're looking for, but when they come across someone clearly looking for something completely different, they don't cut it off. Instead, they spend years and years—the rest of their life, sometimes—trying to prove they can make it work, even though they already know this person doesn't want to move with them toward their goals.

Now, if I had plugged that specific goal into my Life GPS, I would have been able to see a mile away that this relationship was a distraction. Not just for me, but for her as well. And it doesn't apply just to personal relationships. I can't tell you how many times I've invested enormous amounts of valuable time on relationships—personal and professional—that didn't move me closer to my life's goals, simply because I hadn't intentionally plugged those specific addresses into my Life GPS

Now for the last scenario. I had a goal to invest in real estate, to create passive income through rental property. But when someone came by telling me all I had to do was invest $300 on these great products and I'd be sitting on a ton of cash in a year or two, I jumped on it. And ended up out a bunch of cash and the company no longer in business. Here's the thing again, folks: if I had simply been clear in my Life GPS that my goal is to crush it in real estate, there would have been no reason for me to even entertain that opportunity. I would have passed it by in a blink, because I would have recognized it as nothing more than a distraction.

Don't get me wrong; I'm not saying don't multi-task in your life or with your goals. Some of us are fantastic multi-taskers—we can juggle five things at once and never bat an eye. But I want you to understand a concept, one so important that I use it every day in my life.

 Where your focus goes, your energy flows.

That's it. If you want to be dominant in one specific thing, you have to put your focus there. You have no business trying to do a hundred other things around it, because those things will redirect your flow of energy towards them. Clear the decks as much as you can—and still function with a high quality of life—so you can focus on your dream.

I shouldn't have let my focus slip to another area of passive income; it should have been laser-targeted on real estate. The reason I'm so dominant in the real estate field now is because—after that hard-earned lesson—I've put all my focus *specifically* toward mastering all the aspects of owning and flipping rental properties.

You can apply this right now. When you plug that crystal-clear address into your Life GPS, not only will you be able to identify those things that can sidetrack you, but you'll have a much easier time avoiding them. There will be no blur, no hazy line between a good opportunity and a waste of time. You'll be able to see distractions coming and recognize them for what they are. Whatever address you plug in will determine where you are going—even if you put *no* address in.

How do I do that?

Here's a few steps to get you started quieting the wrong directions in your Life GPS so you can plug in the right ones.

1. **Focus on the Noise:** Take some time to be by yourself. Find a place that makes you comfortable— a local coffee shop, your man-cave, a library— wherever you feel most at peace. Once you're there, sit down, quiet your mind, and ask yourself this question: What address or addresses do you currently have in your Life GPS? I'm sure there are a lot in there, and most aren't bringing you closer to your dream. Because whether you know it or not, whatever you have in there is going to determine your life's destinations. Close your eyes and visualize each of these distractions.

2. **Push out the Noise:** Now, I want you to keep your eyes closed and start to push each of those GPS addresses out of your mind. Imagine them in text form, just words describing each, and delete them one-by-one from your GPS screen until the screen is empty.

3. **Plug in the Address:** Now that your GPS is empty, bring your ultimate dream into your mind. This is the *right* address. This is where you want to be, what you want to be doing, what you want to have achieved. Picture it. Now say it, first in your mind, and then out loud. Now picture yourself typing that address into the screen of your Life GPS. Once

it's in there, picture the destination and see yourself there. What do you look like? How have you changed? Do this as often as you need to keep those distractions out and keep you moving in the right direction.

Congratulations! You just took a big step. Those other responsibilities, they're still there. The grass is still going to grow. Your bills are still going to come due. Your obligations are still your obligations. We're going to talk about how to minimize some of those things later when we discuss Dead Zones. But first, we need to learn how to be clear with our goals, so your Life GPS can be clear with its directions.

Seed Principle:

I have a gift inside of me & it needs no instructions on how to grow but it must be planted in the right enviorement to grow!

you are the very thing you choose to be you're just simply in Seed form! Dont plant your seed in the wrong enviorement!

26

CHAPTER 1 REVIEW

The main way to get ahead in life is to have a firm idea of what you want.

1. What are the five most important things you want to accomplish in the next 365 days?

a) __10,000 / mo income__

b) __close cleaning biz__

c) __Reach Gold manager Level__

d) __Purchase new truck__

e) __Be branded as an influencer to help others overcome thought battles.__

2. A GPS cannot chase multiple street addresses at the same time. It can only focus on one address at a time.

Out of the five items you wrote above, which do you believe to not only be the MOST important to achieve but also the accomplishment that will give you the greatest rate of return strategically. (See video on the "Seed Principle")

✱ Don't plant your seed in the wrong enviorement

3. Distractions are the things that cause us to take our eyes off the road. Can you write down 7 things that you feel may get in your way on this journey?

a) __My cleaning biz__

b) _____

c) _____

d) _____

e) _____

f) _____

g) _____

4. How much time a week will you commit to performing the work needed to arrive at your "destination address?"

_____

_____

_____

_____

_____

5. What resources do you feel you will need to get to your "destination address?" (money, connections, coaching, mentoring, accountability partners, education, etc)

mentor to help me

accountability partner

mindset coaching

Social media training

leadership training

6. What unique gifts, talents, skill set, and expertise are you sitting on that can facilitate your success quicker? (See video: Have I check my inventory)

_____

_____

_____

_____

_____

P.S. When you set an address, the GPS gives you an estimated time of arrival so that you have awareness of the potential travel time. This is how you know what resources you may need for the journey. (See video: What do I need for the Road Trip at www.gpsmysuccess.com)

CHAPTER TWO
BE CLEAR WITH YOUR GOALS

It's a lack of clarity that creates chaos and frustration.
Those emotions are poison to any living goal.
- Steve Maraboli

All right; you plugged the correct address into your GPS, and now you're avoiding all those pesky distractions. So, what happens next? That soothing robotic voice comes floating out of your GPS unit, telling you the first direction you need to turn to start driving toward your destination. You pull out of your driveway and turn right, and pretty soon, the next directions are on their way. In fact, if you peek at the GPS screen, you notice that every single direction—from where you are to where you're headed—is already preloaded and waiting to be called out. Pretty amazing, right? You type in the address, and your GPS gives you crystal clear directions: take a left here, take a right there, take another left, and boom! You're at the bank. Ever have it give you vague instructions? You ever find yourself driving down the freeway and your GPS directions sound something like this? "Take the exit ramp on the right in three miles … wait, no … two miles … wait, I was right the first time … oh shoot, go three more miles until you reach a fork in the road and then stop while I try to figure this out."

I'm guessing not. Like everyone else in the world, the worst thing your GPS has likely ever done is try to run you through heavy construction or a temporarily closed-off exit. If it gave you directions as bad as the example above, you'd probably grab it and toss it out the window, right? Me, too. And why is that? Because it's impossible to follow directions that aren't clear.

Why do we do this to ourselves so often? I travel all over and meet all kinds of people. And consistently, everywhere I go, before I get up to speak multiple people come up to me and tell me what they want to accomplish in their lives. They want to increase their personal finances. They want to attend more speaking events. They want to lose a bunch of weight.

Those are all fantastic life goals to achieve, and I'm sure you're thinking of some of your own as you read this. Good! It's important to have goals. We need goals. I still have goals. But goals are vague. Goals are the *address*. You're never going to arrive at that address if you never add clear directions to get there. You must give your Life GPS clear life *instructions* if you want to achieve your life goals.

I'm going to brag on myself for a moment. As of the writing of this book, I've lost more than 30 pounds in the past 30 days. Huge accomplishment for me, and one I've been meaning to get to for a long time. I decided this year was going to be the year to get it done. But I didn't stop there. That was just the goal. I didn't stop at "I'm going to lose a bunch of weight." If I did, that would only be punching the address into my Life GPS. That wouldn't have been enough, and I knew it, because I had done that—and failed—before.

This time, I planned it out. I did the research. I chose the Keto diet. I decided how much I wanted my goal weight to be. I planned my workouts, scheduling them around my life. I visualized the end point, saw myself 30 pounds lighter, and then I did the work. Now here I am, with one more goal checked off the list for me this year. In fact, as I look back over my goals for the year, I can see that I've hit all but two. And as of this writing, I've still got 42 days left to knock them out. You know what? I'm going to. Know how I know? It isn't because of luck, and it isn't because of hard work. Hard work *is* important, but it's not why I'm sitting here 30 pounds lighter. It's because I was clear. Not only did I plug the address into my Life GPS, I typed up the directions, too. There was no vagueness. I knew if I followed the directions, I would get to my destination.

So, let me ask you this question: How clear are you being with your Life GPS? Are you just punching in the address, or are you following up with clear directions? Because as I sit here typing, I can promise you, some of your goals are perched right on your doorstep. They're waiting for you, there for the taking. But if you're not clear about them—if you don't take the time to clearly state what steps you need to take to get from "now" to "goal achieved"—chances are they're going to slip right past you.

Clarify what you are for, not against. This is true power.
- Annie Zalezsak

In the previous chapter, I talked about why it's so important to get clear on what your life goals are—the clearer you are, the easier it will be to achieve. But another concept—much deeper than moving *with* clarity—is that the subconscious mind moves *on* clarity. We won't be actively thinking, every second of the day, about what our goals are and how to get there. That would itself be a distraction. Instead, we must program our subconscious minds to keep heading in the right direction. We do that with clarity.

Why is this so important? Think of your mind as two very distinct and different entities. There's the conscious mind; the part that is aware. You get up in the morning; you're mentally aware that you just put on a red sweater. As you leave the house to go to work or the gym, you're aware that in the lane of traffic to your right is a blue Honda Civic. As you drive down the street and come to a stoplight, you're aware of that stop because you can see the red light. A certain level of awareness with your surroundings is tuned in at all waking moments. That's your conscious mind.

The other part of your mind that I want you to visualize is your subconscious mind. The cool thing is that the subconscious *never sleeps.* It's awake 24/7. Even though you might sleep for eight hours at night, your subconscious mind is still taking in sights, sounds, smells—whatever's around you. Television commercials are specifically designed to target your subconscious mind. Every time you see a car commercial, a pizza commercial, or a beer commercial, the whole job for that ad is to permeate and reprogram your subconscious mind to believe they have the superior product. If you need a car, you head to their dealership. If you're craving a pizza, theirs comes to mind first. If you're a beer drinker, they obviously have the best beer.

If you understand the value of the subconscious mind, how it can direct your actions without you even knowing it, then you can understand why this one tool is so important to moving with clarity.

You were asked in a previous chapter to write out your destination address on your mind's GPS screen and then refer back to it—the reason is that every time you look at where you're headed, you are in essence programming your subconscious mind not only to have an awareness of what you want—which is very important—but to also have clarity about what it looks like. You may notice that when you plug an address into the GPS of your car and drive down the street, the GPS repeats to you where you're headed throughout the course of the trip. It keeps you aware of where you're going and the steps it takes to get there, so you don't lose your way.

The same things apply to your life goals. The more descriptive you are, the better. For those of you with weight-loss goals, *exactly* how much do you want to lose this year? For those struggling with money, *exactly* how much do you want to see yourself gain this year? There is a fine line between clarity and confusion. You can have a goal and still be confused about the directions to get there, because you haven't defined it. You haven't visualized all the steps. You don't know what it looks like or smells like. And if you haven't given the goal that kind of clarity, your subconscious can't direct your actions toward it.

When I bought my first Porsche convertible, I did not just walk into a dealership and say, "I need a car." If that was the case, any car would suffice. Remember, if you don't plug in an address, you won't get there. But I had. When I walked onto that lot, I knew exactly the make, model, age, and mileage I expected in the car I would be leaving with. I knew I wanted a two-seater and I knew the color of the convertible top. I was absolutely certain of everything I wanted before I even left the house. Why? Because if I walked onto that lot without clarity, I would have been making a large purchase decision out of confusion. And confusion is often the very thing that keeps you from getting the results you want.

When it came time for me to lose weight, I didn't just say, "I want to lose a few pounds." If I had started that way and lost only three pounds in a six-month run, there is no way in the world I would have been happy with that result. So, to avoid going to the gym and spending hours over many months trying to transform my body only to have lackluster results, I had to be clear on the result I intended to see at the end of that journey.

The same thing happens with money. I hear people say, "I want to get more money this year." Okay, I'll just grab a five from my pocket and hand it to them. That will satisfy their goal, right? They have more money than they had the day before. But I'm willing to bet that's not what they meant when they said they wanted to see more money in their bank account this year. They probably meant a couple of extra zeros on the end of their bank account balance. They want to see their tax bracket change. If this is you, and you're not clear about what "more money" looks like to you, then your goal is immaterial.

Whatever your goal is, there are going to be resources you will need to help you get from where you're standing to the finish line. But if you're not clear on what the goal is, you can't expect to know what those resources are, much less rely on them to get to where you're trying to go.

Let me give you some examples of the resources you're likely to need.

One is education. When I decided to get serious about real estate, I took courses to give me the knowledge I needed to go from where I was to the other side of the finish line. I also found a mentor and coach.

These are very different entities. A **mentor** is the person who gives you the blueprint or the plan for success on a *specific facet* of what you're trying to accomplish. A **coach** is a person who's with you from start to finish, holding you accountable, checking in and kicking your butt when they see you dragging.

Some goals will require specific financial resources. Another resource—one of the most important—is time. For instance, if you're trying to build a business while you're working 40-50 hours a week at another job, you're going to be pretty limited on the amount of time you can dedicate to your new business. That may work for what you're trying to do, or it may not, but you won't know unless you're clear about what the goal is and the steps to get there.

Moving with clarity also helps you know when it's time to let go of outdated resources. I remember coming into sixth grade and seeing that the old ripped, scuffed textbooks my brothers had before me had been replaced with shiny new ones. The new ones looked different, with a different picture on the cover. I asked my teacher, "What happened to the old textbooks?" She said, "History has evolved and the old textbooks were outdated, so we got these new ones." There was very little value left in the old textbooks.

The same thing will happen to some of the resources you use. They'll become outdated, and their value will diminish. Sometimes you just outgrow them. Many times in my own journey, I've had to let go of a mentor that I had grown beyond—it was nothing against what they provided, but my current level of success had surpassed what they were there to teach me. In that season of my journey, they had become an outdated resource. If I had continued to spend my time with them, it would have been a distraction.

This often happens with organizations. In the beginning they help you out in big ways, but as you evolve the return is no longer worth the effort or time involved in maintaining that connection. If that's the case, the organization is an outdated resource. When you move with a subconscious mind tuned with clarity, you'll be able to identify which resources you need and which ones you need to let go.

How do I do that?

There are many tools out there for setting great goals. I like to use a method called SMART goals. I'm going to use the example of my weight loss and how I mapped it out using the SMART goals method:

1. **S**pecific: You need to drill down as far as you can into the details of what you want to achieve and how you're going to achieve it. I was going to lose a specific amount of weight, in a specific amount of time, using a specific diet and specific workouts.

2. **M**easurable: If you can't measure your goal in some way, how can you be sure you've achieved it? For me, that was simple: 30 pounds. If I don't lose 30 pounds, then I haven't achieved my goal. Be sure you know the method you'll use later to determine whether you've achieved your goals.

3. **A**ttainable: This is pretty straightforward, right? Don't set a goal to be able to fly unassisted: humans physically can't do that. Trying it is probably going to get you killed. Make sure that you're choosing a goal that can be achieved *by you*. That doesn't mean aim for the lowest branch in the tree. Aim high! Stretch yourself. But in mapping out your directions, if there seems to be *no* possible route, you may have selected an impossible goal. I knew I had 30 pounds to lose. There was no doubt in my mind that goal was attainable.

4. **R**elevant: This one is the most difficult to peg down. It can seem a bit vague, but it's not. And it's very important. Think about it like this. Does *this* goal move you closer to your *overall* life goals? Does it serve you in a measurable way? Does it build you up?

    Did you answer any of those with "no"? Then this probably isn't a relevant goal for you. But if you answered "yes," it's probably time to start cooking. Losing weight...yeah, that moves me closer to my life goals, serves me, and builds me up (by trimming me down).

5. **T**imely: Never—I repeat, *never*—set a goal, or a step, or a sub-step, that isn't timed to an expected

completion date. It's really easy to forget this step, but it's crucial. And I bet you already know why: if you don't set a timeframe for your goal, life will almost always get in its way. You'll get bogged down at work, and before you know it, instead of losing 30 pounds you'll have gained 20. Don't do that to yourself. I set a timeframe and stuck with it. 30 pounds, 30 days. Done!

I'm not saying I actively think about every step in this method every time I sit down to map out directions to my goals. But it's a good idea to practice listing them all out in the beginning. Some of you will find the more you use them, the more they tend to internalize, and that's okay. The main thing is that you map out those directions so you can get where you want to go.

CHAPTER 2 REVIEW

1. The opposite of clarity is confusion. A GPS does not operate in confusion; It does its best to give the user crystal clear instructions. This keeps the driver from getting lost. On a scale of 1 to 10, how clear are you currently on the direction you should be moving in? BE HONEST!!!

1   2   3   4   5   6   7   8   9   10

Not Clear	Crystal Clear

2. Can you name at least 5 people that currently have what you want? (They can be famous or not)

_____

_____

_____

_____

_____

3. What will you need to do to connect with them? Can you follow them on social media? It is SUPER IMPORTANT to keep what you want in front of you at all times. We are visual creatures so this is one of the easiest ways to program our subconscious mind to achieve results.

4. Now that you have more clarity over your direction, what or who do you need to put down that's slowing or stopping your growth? I'm talking people, places, social groups, organizations, titles/roles, timewasters, etc. If you're not clear, I will be going into greater detail in Chapter 3.

a) _____

b) _____

c) _____

d) _____

e) _____

P.S. The more clear you are about where you're about to go, the easier it will be for you to get there. You always want to move with clarity because recognizing opportunities and shortcuts will be easier as well. (See video: Taking the shortcut at www.gpsmysuccess.com)

CHAPTER THREE
CONNECTIVITY AND DEAD ZONES

You are only one connection away from anything that
you want; but you must make the <u>right</u> connection.
- Karim R. Ellis

Technology is an amazing thing. Not long ago, people stared up at the stars, measuring the horizon with strange-looking navigational instruments, in order to get where they were going. More recently—and chances are you've been around long enough to remember this—we carried around bulky atlases everywhere we went. And they'd be useless every 2-3 years because the roads had changed so much. Now we have this wonderful thing called GPS, and it is nothing short of a technological marvel.

But do you actually know how it works? I didn't. I had to look it up, and I still don't completely understand it. But what I do understand is that it uses a complex system I like to call the "trifecta." The trifecta consists of a GPS unit (the one on your dash or in your phone), a nearby cell tower, and a satellite orbiting up in space. You plug in an address, the GPS unit pings the local cell tower, the cell phone tower sends a signal to the satellite, and then the satellite maps your G.P.S.-enabled device in real time, giving you step-by-step directions until you reach your destination.

Now, I'm not going to pretend I know how any of that works, but the result of the trifecta is a very important concept. That result is *connectivity*. As long as those three items are talking to each other, you get directions. Simple, and oh, so helpful! Until the connection is lost.

That happened to me recently. A contact of mine had reached out and offered me a big payday to do a speaking event for them. I was so excited! I'd been building this relationship for quite a while, and this event would put me in front of a lot of people. He asked if I had time to catch up and discuss the event, and of course I said yes. But he was *super* old-school. He didn't want to catch up over the phone; he had no idea how to use text messages; an Internet-based conference was completely out of the question. He wanted me to come to his downtown office so we could discuss the event and I could sign all the paperwork. He didn't even have a fax machine. With a payday this big on the line, and with the chance to help as many as 300 people in one sitting, I said, "Yes, sir!" and made the trip.

I was traveling in rush-hour traffic—you probably know where this is going. I'm watching my GPS, focused on staying in my lane, trying not to hit anyone... and I missed my exit. I thought, *No worries, I have GPS It'll recalculate my route, and in a few seconds I'll be on my way again.* But as soon as I missed the exit, I found myself in a "dead zone." I looked down at my phone—*zero* bars. As if I had stepped into somebody's basement or driven into a three-story parking garage. My magical directions device was useless. No signal, no directions. I had to go *miles* down the road before I got a signal again, and was almost late to an important meeting because of it.

That ever happen to you? Not fun, is it? GPS works on connectivity. You type in that address, you get those directions, and as long as there's a good connection between the trifecta, there's a strong chance you're going to get where you want to be.

Your Life GPS is no different; connectivity in this sense refers to people you need to connect with to eventually reach your goals and dreams. Do you know who those are in the upcoming year to get you across the finish line? For me, there are a lot.

Number one on my list is my Heavenly Father. Sometimes I have to change my Global Positioning System into a God Positioning System. There have been moments in my life where I've had to get down on my knees, crawl into my prayer closet, and seek God for instructions. God *always* has a strong signal.

Other times it's been my supporters, my true friends, members of my family who always have my back. People who offer encouragement when I need it most, or give me advice when I can't figure out the next step. I also need strong connections with accountability partners, people who hold my feet to the fire, and vice-versa, to ensure we're each getting things done to plan.

I'm actually amazed how many people *don't* use accountability partners. We've all had them, many of us without realizing it. Every job you ever worked at, there was a boss monitoring your work and making sure you turned in good hours. Mess around and lower your productivity, what happens? Accountability.

So, who's going to be your personal accountability partner as you move into the next year? This is especially important if you're an entrepreneur. It can be hard to get things done with all that new freedom of schedule, unless you have somebody holding your feet to the fire.

Another set of connections I suggest are peers in the environment you wish to excel in. Jim Rohn famously said—I absolutely love this: "Your life will mirror the actions of the five people you hang out with the most." Five! That's huge! So, if I were to jump through the pages of this book right now and grab your cell phone, who will I see on your speed dial? Who fills up your Facebook feed, your Snapchat? Would I find people who will elevate you and bring you to your vision of success? Or people who will drag you down?

And lastly, I would add the concept of the mentor/mentee relationship. Most people get the first half of this concept. They can clearly see the benefit of having a mentor, but they don't see how mentoring someone else is going to help them reach their own dreams. I mean, you're busy, right? How is taking on another responsibility going to help you get to your goals? You might be surprised.

Picture your life as a tall empty glass. You begin to find success, and before you know it, life begins to pour things into that glass. You continue making strides toward your personal ambitions, and pretty soon, that life glass is full to the rim.

But hey, people still recognize you, right? You're "the guy," and people continue to bring you opportunities; only now, there's no room for anything else inside your glass. So, what happens then? Do you drive yourself, and your loved ones, crazy taking on more responsibilities than you can really handle? Or, maybe you let those opportunities spill out onto the floor and go to waste.

Here's another solution, one I've been practicing for some time now. Once my glass is so full there's no room left to take on any additional responsibilities, I begin to seek out people who are coming down the same path I've been on, and I start pouring into *their* glasses. And what I've found is, if I pour into their glasses, the level of my own glass goes down, allowing other mentors space to pour from their glasses into mine. There's zero waste; more opportunities can flow to me while I'm creating more opportunities for others. And you find out pretty quickly that when everyone wins, you win.

It isn't just big, life-changing, can't-miss-out opportunities you can share. It's a lot like tithing; you can offer your time, your effort, your wisdom, and you'll find others are eager to offer these things to you as well.

So, as you move forward with your goals, who are you going to seek out as a mentor? And maybe more importantly, who are you going to take under your wing? Who are you going to grab by their belt strap and say, "Here, let me help you up to the next level?" Because what you make happen for others, God will always make happen for you.

Remember earlier I mentioned dead zones? Those happen in your Life GPS, too. And just like when you lose the signal when entering a dead zone driving in your car, dead zones in life are breakdowns in connectivity and you lose your way. So, what are these "dead zones?"

Let's start by looking at your friends—the people you hang with. Do you give time to some who aren't lifting you up? Just because they can give you a slick high-five and start talking jive doesn't mean you can depend on them on your way up the mountain.

I live by the philosophy that my life is a dictatorship, not a democracy. I'm the CEO of my life, and I reserve the right to hire and fire people from it as I see fit. If I perceive you're going do anything to slow me down in my pursuit of success, I will flat-out let you go. Does that sound harsh? A little too selfish? Let me ask you: how many times have you been unable to meet the needs of those people who *do* lift you up, because you're too busy spending time on the ones who *don't*? Many of us hang onto the bottom-feeders in our lives, the ones we should've let go yesteryear. Those people are dead zones. When we're around them, we lose our way to our goals.

The second dead zone I want you to watch out for—I want to be upfront with you about this—is your family. A blood tie does not automatically mean they have your best interest at heart. The fact is, most of the struggles that took me off my game were with family. Now, that doesn't mean call up all your relations and tell them you're MIA until you reach all your dreams. It just means pay attention to how you spend your time. You're chasing big goals, and if you want to reach them you *must* keep your guard up.

The third dead zone, for some of you, may be your job. I'm not necessarily saying you have to hate your job for it to be a dead zone. When I parted from my 9-to-5 and jumped over to the entrepreneur side of things, it wasn't because I hated my work. A lot of people do. I hear all kinds of stories from people who can't stand their jobs; that's not my story. I didn't leave my job because I hated the boss, the work, or the pay (though that could've been better). I left my job because it was a dead zone. There was no growth potential toward my dreams. I wasn't mastering skills that would serve me toward my goals. It was just a paycheck. J-O-B: Just Over Broke. They paid me just enough to stay attached, and I worked just hard enough to keep them from saying, "We're going let you go,"...until they did.

Now this was only a job; there are millions out there. But there is a lack of people who know how to chase their goals and dreams. I was spending 40 hours a week watering a dream seed that did not belong to Karim Ellis. That seed belonged to my boss, and his boss, all the way up to the owner of the company. Once I figured that out, I immediately began to plan how I could take those 40 hours per week and invest them in steps that would further the dreams of Karim the Entrepreneur.

Organizations can be another dead zone. In the last year I have let go of probably 10 to 12 different organizations. I'm not saying these aren't valuable organizations; just the opposite. They all do good things for the community in one way or another. Each of them served a purpose for me during one season of my life. But once that season was over, they became timewasters. When I go to an organizational meeting and begin to network only to find there's no growth going on inside of me, that's when it's time to leave. It's like a tree. It's obvious when a tree is dead, because it no longer grows; it no longer produces leaves, flowers, fruit. Some of us stay in organizations out of habit. We keep showing up because it's what we always do on a Thursday night, not realizing that we stopped producing fruit a long time ago. That valuable time could be spent doing something else which moves you toward your goals.

Another dead zone can be your education. There was a time in my life when I thought that to be a professional speaker, I had to have a PhD behind my name and all sorts of accolades, and if I didn't have those things, I couldn't move forward. Because of that, I delayed moving toward my destiny for a long time. You may have felt similar hesitations in your path, may have let the lack of education slow you down. But one of the things I have realized in my life is that what God has destined *for* you he will manifest *in* you. He will not give you a goal or a dream to go after and not give you the resources for it. You already have a box full of tools just waiting to be used, and you don't even know they're there. So, the question is this: what's inside your toolbox? What are you sitting on *right now* that you can use to move toward your dreams? I often speak to large rooms, and every time I know I'm in front of a crowd of folks who are packed with gifts and talents and expertise. But because they don't know the value of what they're sitting on, they believe they need more before they can start moving toward their own personal finish line. But God is not going to give you a mission without giving you the tools. Those tools may be internal—meaning your gifts and talents or level of expertise in your field. They may also be external— God may present specific connections to you, which can open doors and present opportunities.

The last dead zone I'll mention is your environment. It's always amazing to me how few people realize just how powerful the environment around them is at helping them create success or holding them back from it. If you want to grow an oak tree, you must plant an acorn in the ground, right? But it's not enough for you to simply plant it; for it to grow properly, it has to be planted in the proper soil. Too wet, and it will rot. Too dry, and it will never begin to form.

Most of us take our dream seed—essentially *ourselves*—and plant it in toxic soil. Then we get upset when we don't see that growth or success we envisioned for ourselves. **You can't grow in bad soil.** There have been many times in my life where I've had to reach down into the ground and get my hands dirty, to replant myself in an environment that was better suited for me to reach my goals. When I got serious about investing in real estate, I surrounded myself with real estate investors. When I got serious about being a kick-butt speaker, I surrounded myself with mentors who could help me toward that end. What environment will be most conducive to the success of your growth toward your goals? Where do you need to plant that dream seed? You will eventually conform to your environment. Don't plant your seed in less-than-fertile soil.

How do I do that?

To make steady progress toward the SMART goals you've identified in your life, you're going to have to keep your Life GPS working optimally. And that means maintaining connectivity and avoiding dead zones. Here's a few tips I use:

Connectivity:

1. **Evaluate What You've Got:** Grab a pen and a piece of paper or open a document on your computer or notetaking app and make a list of all the big supporters in your life. These could be your God, specific family members or friends, co-workers who get what you're doing, your spouse.

2. **Evaluate What You Need:** Dig deep here and be really honest with yourself. What are your weaknesses? Where do you need support? What areas of your dream look like vague clouds in your head? Now, who do you know that you could have a better relationship with and might be able to help you with some of these blind spots? Who is a local guru in the industry of your dreams that you could reach out to and start building a relationship? Could they become a mentor of yours?

3. **Reach Out:** Now that you have your lists, start with those connections you already have and be open with them. Tell them what you're trying to achieve. If you need help, ask them. Don't let your pride get in the way. The worst they can say is "no." Keep those relationships in the forefront of your mind and never let them slip. Next, reach out to the second list. Set up lunches. Ask common acquaintances to make introductions. Cold call if you must, but be ready to be open and up front with them. Tell them who you are and what you're doing. You'd be surprised how many people are just waiting for opportunities to help others move down a path they've already been down.

4. **Be Flexible:** This is not a static list that you write up and never update. It is absolutely going to change, and that is really important. Some people you thought you could rely on will flake out on you. Don't sweat it. Keep being true to yourself and your dreams. You'll also come to points on your journey where your needs change. Be ready to re-

configure the list of people who can help you fill in the new missing pieces as you move forward.

Dead Zones:

5. **Take Stock:** Still got that pen and paper handy? I'm just kidding. Don't start writing people and organizations down in a list just to strike a line through their names. That's the kind of thing that'll get a person wrongly convicted of a crime. But, do take some time to evaluate the "whos" and "whats" that are holding you back—the dead zones in your life.

6. **Where Are You?** Now, think about what's going on around you. Is your job propelling you toward your goal? Is the environment around you setting you up for success? Don't allow yourself to dodge these questions. If you answered "no," it's time to do some major life planning. I'm not saying to call your boss right after you finish reading this paragraph, or text your wife and tell her you want to move across the country. As I've mentioned before, you've got to have clear, well-planned directions if you want to get where you're trying to go. Take some time to figure out whether there are changes— small ones or big ones—you can work toward with the help of your connections.

CHAPTER 3 REVIEW

1. Name 5 people in relation to your GPS destination address that you know you should now be connected with.

a) _____

b) _____

c) _____

d) _____

e) _____

2. Name 3 organizations you can join that can help push you closer to your GPS destination address.

a) _____

b) _____

c) _____

3. Do you have a coach/mentor and are they mentoring you in the arena SPECIFIC to your GPS destination address?

_____

_____

_____

_____

4. Are you pouring out your accumulated wisdom through mentoring to others? Sometimes giving to others is the quickest way to receive. (see video on: My Cup Runneth Over at www.gpsmysuccess.com)

DEAD ZONE TALK
5. Honesty moment. What's holding you back? Name as many personal dead zones as you can. Remember, you cannot conquer what you refuse to confront.

_____

_____

_____

_____

_____

_____

6. Are you fully committed to escaping your dead zones? And if so, why?

_____

_____

_____

_____

_____

_____

CHAPTER FOUR
LEARN TO RECALCULATE

Be shapeless, formless, like water. When you pour water in a cup, it becomes the cup. When you pour water in a bottle, it becomes the bottle. When you pour water in a teapot, it becomes the tea pot. Water can drip and it can crash.
Become like water, my friend.
\- Bruce Lee

Doesn't it feel good to be out of those dead zones, to feel the connectivity now? Excellent! Nothing feels better than being on your way with a clear set of directions in hand. But what happens when you run into an accident on the highway? You've been there a million times, right? You're driving along, trying to get to the bank or the grocery store. Maybe you're heading out on vacation, you've just accelerated up the on-ramp and gotten up to speed, and *boom!*—a slow-down. Red lights stretch as far as the eye can see.

But you don't sweat it, because you've got your trusty GPS sitting right next to you and it's already saying those most important words, "recalculating route." Your little navigational sidekick does its magic, and in a few moments you're tracking down a new path to your destination.

In life, any number of things can pop up to distract, block, sidetrack, and effectively discourage us from continuing on toward our goal. And so many dreams are laid to rest because someone didn't know how to chart a new course and keep on moving.

I run into "wrecks" in my life all the time. Just recently I had to deal with a distraction. Now this wasn't a super-important goal, but it was a goal nonetheless. You see, I have a thing for Porsche convertibles. Ever since I was a kid I've considered them the ultimate car, and for as long as I can remember I have dreamed of owning one. I've been blessed—I bought an all-white Porsche with a blue convertible top. I call it the White Lotus.

I bought this car on Friday night and my best friend was having his birthday party on Saturday evening. I was so excited. I had wanted this car for so long, and now I had a chance to break it out in style. I wanted so bad to just show up at my friend's party and shock the crowd with how beautiful it was. I didn't tell anybody; it was going to be a big surprise. I'd planned it all out. I'd to show up at 6 o'clock with the windows down, top back, music blaring, and my Ray-Bans on, and just watch mouths drop.

Now, the Porsche was a bit dirty on the outside, and I wasn't happy with the condition the dealership had turned it over to me in, so I left early, took the car to a professional detailing service at 4 o'clock, paid $300, and got that car looking like new money. I zoomed out onto the highway, and right away, this cherry red Mustang comes barreling up the next on-ramp. I had to jump on my brakes to avoid getting hit.

So, I slowed down and was cruising behind this car, and I noticed there were four teenagers in the car. One of them probably just got their driver's license and took Daddy's ride out for a spin. They're horsing around, reaching back, slapping at each other, creating a big distraction, just acting like kids.

Then it happened. No, it wasn't a wreck. Thankfully, this isn't that kind of story.

One of the kids in the backseat rolled the window down and, at 70 miles per hour, hurled his Giant Guzzler Slurpee cup out the window—surely thinking he could throw this thing hard enough it would somehow land safely on the side of the highway. Here's the thing: this young knucklehead didn't, and likely still doesn't, understand the laws of physics. So, what actually happened is the cup caught the wind, the wind caught the lid, and in a split-second my beautifully detailed white Porsche convertible was covered in very sticky purple Slurpee.

I'm a Christian man. I profess my faith. I love me some Jesus. But I slipped that day. I think I told Jesus to get out of the car, because I was about to handle some business that didn't involve him. It turned into a high-speed chase in 1.5 seconds.

I flew up next to them, shouting every four-letter word under the sun, and they sped up, eyes wide, just trying to escape the psycho in a white, blue, and now purple Porsche. It lasted for several miles, and—I'm not proud to admit—I missed my exit, and even sped off in the wrong direction for a bit.

But the voice of reason did finally take over. My inner voice finally registered, saying, "Karim, you let these kids go. You were a kid once, too, and you did some nonsense in your day. Besides, it's the weekend; if you get arrested today you won't get out till Monday."

So, I let them go. I calmed down. But now I was late for the party and had a Slurpee-covered car. Now, I'm torn whether to even go to the birthday or just grab my towel and go home.

I remember pulling up my GPS and punching in directions to go home. And something odd happened. As I tried to type in the directions, my GPS went goofy; it kept saying "recalculating... recalculating..." and wouldn't take my directions. Something switched in me; I took it as a sign from God to continue on with the mission and go to the party.

So, I found a gas station—when you're involved in a 40-minute chase at 80 miles per hour, you're gonna burn through some gas. I found a cheap $3 carwash to get the Slurpee off, and I made my way to the party. I didn't get there the way I'd wanted to, so I had to change my plans a little; I had to recalculate. I showed up at the end, put the top down, turned the music up and everybody got to celebrate my new ride as they came out of the party.

Sometimes life has a funny way of simply "happening," and it doesn't always "happen" for your benefit. Sometimes it will put a frown on your face, and sometimes it will make you cry. So, what's your response going to be? Maybe life's throwing curveballs at you as you read this. Maybe you're dealing with financial challenges. Maybe you're on the verge of losing your house or your car. Maybe you are dealing with health crises. Maybe a divorce or breakup is imminent. Maybe you or a family member are dealing with substance abuse. Friend, I feel for you. Those things aren't easy, and nobody can tell you otherwise. But what are you going to do about it? When life gives you that one-two punch designed to put you on your back, will you fold? Or will you look around yourself, take stock of your circumstances, and allow your Life GPS to recalculate?

I can't tell you how many times I've had to recalculate my life to get to the finish line. And most of us can relate. We start on the journey thinking there's only one way to achieve our dreams, not knowing that there are multiple avenues and multiple routes to get to the finish line. I love this quote by Bruce Lee; he said, "Your job is to be formless like water." Let that sink in for a second. Water is flexible. Water is adaptable. Water is formless. Water finds a way to get to its destination. And if you make yourself formless like water, if you commit to being able to recalculate when life throws an obstacle in your path, you'll find a way to get down that mountain to the finish line. When I get stuck in a traffic jam, my GPS doesn't say "you're stuck." It starts to give me alternative routes to get me from where I am to where I want to be. There's always more than one way. Are you willing to recalculate?

> *There's more than one way to do things.*
> *There's always different points of views*
> *and styles of pitching.*
> - Tim Hudson

There is always more than one way to the finish line. When I originally started this entrepreneurial journey, my main focus was on making money. I was living paycheck-to-paycheck. My lifestyle was a system of staying one step ahead of the bill collectors. I was living month-to-month, and I routinely had more month in my year than money to last me. But as I got clarity, I quickly realized that the first goal for me to get out of that grind was just getting an extra $5,000 in the bank. That's not a lot of money now in the grand scheme of things. But back then, with a job paying $14 per hour, it felt like a big cushion.

So, my first entrepreneurial adventure was flipping vintage video games from the early 2000's. I would take my paycheck on Friday, go online—eBay mostly—and buy box-lots of toys from my childhood that other kids had left behind. I would find parents whose kids had moved on to college and left behind messy bedrooms with boxes of old toys. I would spend anywhere from $100 to $200 on these boxes. Parents saw them as valueless junk they just wanted to get rid of. Some, I would slap on a fresh coat of paint. I would tighten up the screws if they needed it, and then I would put those toys back on eBay at a huge markup.

It was an immediate success. People pay a lot of money for nostalgia. Before I was selling toys, I collected toys from my childhood, because my childhood was a much happier time in my memory. I remember buying an original 1984 Optimus Prime one time in pretty great condition on eBay for $25. All the pieces were intact. I cleaned him up, slapped a little paint on him, and sold him to a collector for $350.

Pretty soon, I was making more money selling vintage toys online than I was from my 9-to-5. I had money literally rolling in, and had built up a nice little nest egg. And I just knew in the bottom of my heart that I was going to be this crazy online toy millionaire, because the cash flow that season was just awesome.

And then out of nowhere it started to slow down and I had to stop. I hadn't realized that the toy companies—

Hasbro and all the rest from the 80s—had started paying attention. They saw all these old toys, no longer in circulation, were beginning to make all this money in the auction and resale markets, so they did something I never saw coming. They pulled out those old molds and reproduced, in limited quantities, those old toys. I faced a dilemma: I could still find the old 1980's Optimus Prime and straighten him up a little, but someone who wanted that famous toy from their childhood could now go to any major toy store and find the same action figure on the shelf at only a *slightly* higher markup, but in much better condition. I lost a lot of business, seemingly overnight.

Here's the deal, though: at that point, I'd already been fired from my job. I hadn't even minded being fired at first, because I was making more money online. I had no desire to work for someone else. But when the toy market changed course, I had no choice but to recalculate as well.

Sometimes you have to recalculate by force rather than by choice. We talked earlier about *choosing* to recalculate—meaning there's more than one way to reach the finish line and you just pick the best one. But sometimes it's not even an option, but a necessity to stay above water. So, what I want to tell you is this: **Don't get so stuck on what you're currently doing in this season, that you're not open to switching lanes.** That's critically important. The destination can remain the same, but the lane you take there—or the route, or the type of vehicle—can change anytime *and still get you there.*

If you're driving on a highway and suddenly the first three lanes back up, you have options. You can choose to stay in the slow lane, or you can merge into the fast lane. It doesn't change where you're headed. You're still going to get to where you intended to go; you've simply adjusted what lane you're going to use to get there.

So, when the toy business lane came to a complete standstill, I hopped into the real estate investing lane and began learning how to flip houses instead. The amount of money I wanted in my bank account didn't change, only the tools and resources I would use to get there. I could have stayed online and watched my financial life die a slow and inglorious death because I refused to stop selling toys when that business was no longer profitable. Or, I could choose to lick my wounds, hop into another lane, and understand that all I was doing was recalculating how I got to the finish line.

Something wonderful happened along the way. As I began to get savvy at flipping houses, I started to run into a lot of people who wanted to learn how to do the same thing. People who had been following my journey online. So now not only was I making money flipping houses, but also making money teaching other real estate investors. And then something else miraculous happened. I was asked to come speak at different venues, because they loved the *motivational* aspect of my message. Before I knew it, I was getting paid to give powerful, game-changing keynote speeches across the country and around the world. Then a book was released, and then coaching programs went out, and I had multiple streams of income that made getting to that $500K income finish line more achievable than ever before. Remember, the destination does not change. But I could have missed my mark if I hadn't been willing to recalculate, from selling toys to real estate and then professional speaking. Sometimes a recalculation is *absolutely necessary* to get you to your fantastic finish line.

I've said it before, and I'll say it again: **the goal is to get you to the finish line**. Do not get to hung up on the vehicle God uses to help you get there. Because the lane can change at any time.

How do I do that?

Setbacks can sting and take the wind out of your sails. But the reality is that no dream gets achieved without them. You must be able to recalculate if you're going to finish strong. Here's how I do it:

1. **Stop and Breathe:** Most of the time, the situation isn't nearly as bad as it seems. Pull the car over and get your mind right. Don't go chasing after a bunch of kids on the highway. Breathe and realize that your dream is still right there, waiting for you to continue the journey.
2. **Remember Your "Why":** Why is this dream so important to you? Is if for your health? Is it for financial freedom? Is it for personal fulfillment? Focus on your "why," and you'll find the obstacles in your way will shrink in comparison to it.
3. **Phone a Friend:** Remember those accountability partners? Now is the time to test their worth. Call one up and level with them. Tell them what's going on, and get some perspective from somewhere outside the situation at hand. Even if they don't have a ready solution for you, often simply describing the situation out loud can illustrate that it isn't the major setback you initially thought.

CHAPTER 4 REVIEW

1. In life, things will happen that slows us down. On the road it may be a traffic jam, and accident, or a road closure. We must remember that temporary delay does not mean permanent denial.

What is the last major delay you faced in life?

_____

_____

_____

_____

2. How did you choose to handle it?

_____

_____

_____

_____

3. Is there anything you could have done differently now that you have awareness on the topic?

_____

_____

_____

_____

4. What are some of the ways you can prepare yourself against potential setbacks on your current journey? For instance, I have a mentor/coach in place to help me when I travel in to unknown territory to hasten my learning curve on the journey. I have sufficient cash reserves set asides in case of unexpected financial challenges. I spend a lot of time making strategic connections in the arena that I'm dominating in. These are few examples.

_____

_____

_____

_____

_____

P.S. Recalculating means that my focus is still on the destination despite any unforeseen slowdowns.

CHAPTER FIVE
CHECK YOUR HISTORY LOG

Your history tells me where you've been.
Learn from it or repeat it. The choice is yours.
- Karim R. Ellis

I have a friend who got caught cheating on his wife about four years ago. Have you ever been through something like that with a friend? It's devastating. You love the guy, but you wish you could go back in time and wring their neck. *What were you thinking?*

And not only did he do this terrible thing, but you'll never guess how he ended up getting caught. I can see the thought bubbles forming over your head right now. She must have got hold of his cell phone, right? Nope. Came home smelling like perfume? Nope. She found a text message, an email, lipstick on his collar? Did she get access to his social media account? Did someone catch them out in the streets? Nope, nope, and nope! This man got caught cheating because of the GPS.

This family had two vehicles. A four-door sedan and an SUV. The SUV would be deemed the "shared car." This means the car usage would alternate depending on the specific need. So, my friend came home one day and told his wife that his job had picked up a new client, which meant mandatory overtime for the next three or four months. He would be coming home late in the evenings, and there would be weekends where she wouldn't see him at all. And his wife was so trusting, she thought nothing of it. She loved this man so deeply, she completely trusted him.

But this woman also loved antique shopping. And being left alone more than usual, she decided to take the share car and head over to this great antique shop she had visited a few months back. The only problem was, she couldn't remember the name. She Googled it and still couldn't figure it out, and was about ready to give up when she remembered that when she had visited it before someone had told her the name of the shop, and she had put it and the address inside the GPS of the share car. So, she walked out to the garage, started up the SUV, fired up the GPS, and accessed the history log.

She found the antique shop, but she also found a lot of other addresses that she didn't recognize. Very expensive five-star restaurants; really fun places like movie theaters, putt-putt golf, and laser tag. She also found the addresses of very expensive hotels. She had been to none of these places. He was cooked.

I'm not telling you this story so you can close this book and tell your friends Karim Ellis taught you how to cheat on your spouse without getting caught. That's not what this is about.

But let me ask you this: if I were to ask you to hand over your Life GPS right now, what would I find in its history log? Would I find you've been cheating on your goals and dreams? Would I find it full of destinations that fit everybody else's agenda?

You see the destinations in your Life GPS history log show where you've been spending all your focus. And where your focus goes your energy flows, remember?

Now I want you to listen in real close to this; there's a reason I saved this one for last. The truth is, most people aren't unsuccessful because they didn't put an address in the GPS. Most people know where they want to go. Most people aren't unsuccessful because they don't have clarity about what they want to achieve. And it isn't usually because they aren't connected with the right people, or because they're stuck in some dead zone. It isn't even because they don't know how to recalculate themselves to get to the finish line.

All of those things are important. All of those things derail people from achieving their dreams. But they aren't the *biggest* problem.

The #1 reason why people don't achieve greatness in their life is because **they spend their time cheating on their own goals and dreams with everybody else's**. They get so caught up in trying to live up to everyone else's standards that they forget about their own.

What addresses fill up your Life GPS history log right now? What addresses have you been haunting all year long that have kept you from getting your own dreams off the ground? It's time for a purge.

> *The chains of habit are too light to be felt*
> *until they are too heavy to be broken.*
> - Bertrand Russell

I've heard it said many times by scientists that it takes 21 days to make something a habit, and only 90 days to turn that habit into a lifestyle. So I want to go deeper here for a second, because in the first part of this chapter we talked about history logs, and how a lot of people miss their mark because their log is filled with addresses that have nothing to do with getting them to their fantastic finish line.

So, here's a question for you. When's the last time you thought about some of your current habits?

One of the biggest problems with the concept of habits is that a lot of the time we only think of *known* habits. Specifically, destructive ones—the big ones. We think about people who have an alcohol or drug abuse habit, or a sex addiction habit. Those are the ones we hear about regularly on social media and through media channels like the news.

But I want to tell you that your life is governed and dictated by *all* your habits. That's right, all of them. I have sat in many a room and told people that if I can identify your habits, I can predict your future. Because your habits let me know what you've been doing for a lifetime.

If someone has a perpetual habit of being lazy, I pretty much know whether or not that person will be successful in their goal to lose weight, or a goal of quitting drinking. I'm not saying it's a deadlocked sure thing, but the chances of that person pulling off a major change are not good— because they have a habit standing in their way. If, on the other hand, they have a habit of getting stuff done, then they are much more likely to achieve that goal, whatever it might be.

But let's go even deeper on this with another question. When's the last time you had to physically *think* about how to tie your shoe? When's the last time you had to *think* about how to hold a spoon, or a knife, or a fork, or a cup, or a glass? When's the last time you *thought* about how to physically take a drink of something? And if you're a seasoned driver, when's the last time you *thought* about how you hold your hand on the steering wheel while you're driving?

I'm willing to bet that with each of these things you probably take for granted now, you actually had to focus during that initial 21-day learning cycle. You had to physically look at your shoes while you tied that knot for the first several times, so you understood how to do the loop and the bow. When you held a spoon or fork for the first time as a toddler, you probably gripped it with a full fist; then, as you got more comfortable, you learned to use your index finger and your middle finger and maybe your thumb to balance the spoon. And if you're a seasoned driver, you probably don't even think a lot when you drive. Your hands are one on the wheel or on the radio, or you might be on the phone (hands-free of course), because now, driving is a habit to you. It doesn't require a lot of concentration.

You don't think about those things anymore, because driving, all those other examples I gave you, and a plethora more, are habits now. You spent the 21 days and capped them off with 90. You didn't even know it at the time, but by the time you were done, you had formed habits and built them into lifestyles. You've done them so many times that those particular things in your life are on autopilot.

Well guess what, folks—those are only the tangible things. We didn't talk about the intangible. We covered it a little bit earlier when we talked about laziness and procrastination. Those are the intangible habits a lot of us have. They show up in our life at an early age, and the more we entertain them, they can easily become habits that disrupt the flow of our success.

But those aren't the only things that can become a habit. A habit is anything that is well-ingrained, well-entrenched, done so many times that you do it on instinct. For example, when I begin to sneeze, I throw my hand up to block the sneeze. That's instinct. Because I've done it so many times.

I want you to be careful that the everyday addresses you find yourself putting into your Life GPS are not forming habits as well.

One of the things that used to hold me down was the habit of never telling people "no." I have a goal. I have a dream. But much like my buddy who got caught cheating on his wife, with all the different addresses, my problem was always saying "yes" to everything. Whatever anyone asked me to do, I found myself doing it, even if it was distracting me from getting to my finish line. I had the habit of not saying "no," and the result was I discovered my Life GPS was full of addresses to everyone else's goals and agendas—not by force, but by choice. My GPS stayed full of addresses that never belonged to me.

This is why I encourage you to actually sit down with whoever you choose as an accountability partner and make a good list of anything you've been doing on a regular basis for the last six months—I mean *anything* you've done that squanders time or takes some amount of time away from your dreams. You may notice patterns in the list. If you can identify your patterns, you can see your habits. And if you can identify your habits, you can also predict your future.

If you're not careful, you'll find that your history log is filled with places that have nothing to do with your goals and dreams. But even more dangerous, you'll discover that you've been *programming yourself* to do these things by habit. That's not where you want to be when it comes to chasing and achieving your goals and dreams. Begin now, identifying and breaking those habits that choke up your history log and keep you from your finish line.

How do I do that?

It's easy to get bogged down in other people's goals, dreams, struggles, drama. And I'm not suggesting you avoid other people and withhold your help from them. I am suggesting that you don't allow that to be your norm. Don't let that sidetrack you from handling your own business. Here are some strategies I use to keep my eyes on the prize:

1. **Have Check-ins with Yourself:** If you want results, you have to be intentional. That means scheduling time by yourself to evaluate what's going on in your life. Have the wrong addresses begun creeping into your GPS log? Don't let it get you down; recalculate and move forward.

2. **Get a Second Opinion:** Who knows you best? Is it your wife, husband, a close friend? Ask them how they think things are going. Have they noticed any changes in you recently? One of the signs I'm getting bogged down with wrong addresses is I start to feel overwhelmed. But I don't notice it first—my wife does. Find that trusted person and see what they have to say.

3. **Pause Before You Commit:** Remember the "life glass" analogy? You've got a full glass, my friend.

When something comes along vying for your already taxed time, pause before accepting it. Determine whether it's something you want to try to cram into your life right then. Maybe it isn't worth it. Maybe it is an opportunity for you to pour into someone else's glass. Never be afraid to say "No."

CHAPTER 5 REVIEW

1. The history log gives you a great level of insight into where you have been spending most of your time. Can you honestly write down 5 ways you've been spending a majority of your time in the last 365 days based on your current history log?

a) _____

b) _____

c) _____

d) _____

e) _____

2. Are you satisfied with what you see? If not, what addresses do you need to stop inputting immediately? What's the pattern you notice from looking at your history log?

_____

_____

_____

_____

_____

P.S. Where you've been in the past can be a great indicator of where you're going in the future if you don't recognize the pattern of how and what you spend your time chasing.

SUMMARY

The main reason I wrote this book is to stress the importance of starting your journey to greatness by setting a vision of what you want. It's my belief that I could've gotten my current level of success much faster if I knew where I was going at the age of 18. That a lot of the self-imposed detours would have taken less of a toll because I would've been moving with awareness while keeping an eye out for opportunity. You have been equipped at this point with a powerful road map to help you travel on your journey. I would encourage you to not only share this book with others, especially younger adults but I also challenge you to re-read the material once a year. A year from today you will look at the pages with different insight and wisdom as you have been growing in the right direction.

If you have not joined the Takeoff Academy, I would encourage you to visit www.thetakeoffacademy.com. The site contains coaching, mentoring, education, and many other items that will facilitate your journey to success. The last thing I will mention is this:

The two most valuable resources you will always have are both your mind and your time. When properly fed, nurtured and programmed the human mind can achieve just about anything. It just needs the right information to absorb and process. However the things you put your mind to will always be mirrored in time. Meaning, once time runs out... the game is over.

The Takeoff Academy is a great resource to not only shape your mind but save time on your journey with tips, tricks and shortcuts that facilitate getting to the top of the mountain quicker.

Closing thought:

The address you decide to place inside your life's GPS will determine your destination. It's up to you to figure out where you want to go. Be Blessed!!!

ABOUT THE AUTHOR

Karim R. Ellis is a Dynamic Powerhouse Speaker with over 10 years of experience in the field of speaking, training, coaching and breakthrough success. As the author of the "GPS My Success", Karim takes great pride in developing both leaders and champions. His messages and concepts help people to grow to the next level as he inspires an atmosphere of greatness in the lives he connects with on a daily basis.

Karim is also a member of the National Speakers Association, Past President with Toastmasters International and is the owner of two successful businesses for 20 years.

As a member of the John Maxwell Team and as a Les Brown Platinum Speaker and protégé, Karim speaks, inspires, and teaches Leadership / Professional Development principles to 60-70 organizations a year. Some of these companies include...

Ford Motor Company, Honda, General Electric, Toyota, Anthem, Kroger, The United States Postal Service, ODOT, The Dept. of Defense DFAS, The United States Military, The National Urban League, SHRM and a host of many more.

All successful organizations understand that effective leadership is at the heart of every business and the Les Brown Institute as well as the John Maxwell Team prides itself on Leadership Creation and Development. As a trainer/ coach, Karim has several engaging group programs specifically designed to take Leaders to the Next Level.

When Karim delivers a message, he absolutely makes sure that the room "gets it". If you are ready for a fun, engaging, entertaining, and inspiring motivational speaker that will leave you amazed... Karim R. Ellis is definitely it!!!

To inquire on booking Karim for your upcoming event please use the contact information below.

Website: www.karimellis.com
Email: info@karimellis.com

CPSIA information can be obtained
at www.ICGtesting.com
Printed in the USA
LVHW081915100320
649619LV00008B/90